STARTERS
ACTIVITIES

Seasons

Macdonald Educational

About Starters Activities

These books cover a variety of activities for children at school or at home. The projects with their step-by-step illustrations, require the minimum of help from teachers or parents. Most of the words in the text will be in the reading vocabulary of the majority of young readers. Word and sentence length have also been carefully controlled. Extra information and more complex activities are included at the end of each book. Where possible, the child is free to invent and experiment on his own, but concise instructions are given wherever necessary. Teachers and experts have been consulted on the content and accuracy of these books.

Illustrated by: Geoff Hocking

Managing Editor: Su Swallow

Editor: Diana Finley

Production: Stephen Pawley, Vivienne Driscoll

Reading consultant: Donald Moyle, author of The Teaching of Reading and senior lecturer in education at Edge Hill College of Education

Chairman, teacher advisory panel: F. F. Blackwell, director of the primary extension programme, National Council for Educational Technology

Teacher panel: Stephanie Connell, Sally Chaplin, Margaret Anderson

Colour reproduction by:
Colourcraftsmen Limited

Filmsetting by:
Layton-Sun Limited

© Macdonald and Company
(Publishers) Limited 1974
ISBN 0 356 04928 0
Made and printed in Great Britain by:
Purnell & Sons Limited, Paulton, nr Bristol

First published in 1974 by
Macdonald Educational
St Giles House
49-50 Poland Street
London W1

Contents

Spring

Make a weather house out of card.
Keep a record of the weather each day.
How often has the sun been out?

1

Plants begin to grow in the spring.
Collect some small branches or twigs
with big buds.
Put them in jars.

2

Keep the jars by a window.
The buds will soon begin to grow.
Which buds grow the fastest?

paper tissues

cotton wool

hair

feathers

wool

string

In spring birds make nests,
ready for their eggs.
You can help them.

4

Put out some of these things.
Which things do the birds choose first
for their nests?

5

coconut shy

hoopla

lucky dip

Summer
You could have a summer fair
for all your friends.

6

Punch and Judy

fortune teller

skittles

Here are some stalls and games
you could have at the fair.
You could make things to eat, too.

7

You might go to the beach.
You might have a sandpit.
Here are some things you can do
in the sand.

8

Build a big sandcastle.
Decorate it with things you find.
Make some pictures in the sand.
Use stones and plants to help you.

Find things you like on the beach.
Then you can use them to make a
wall-hanging.

10

See if you can find
a piece of fishing net.
You could also use an old net curtain.
Thread things through the net.

11

Autumn

Autumn is harvest time.
You could have a harvest festival
of your own.

12

Collect berries, nuts and leaves.
Sort your things into colours.
Ask your friends to come and look.

You could give a Halloween party.
Ask every one to dress up.
Make masks and lanterns for the party.
14

Make an apple-bobbing game
to play with your friends.
Float some apples in a tub of water.
Then try to eat the apples.

Long ago people made corn dollies
at harvest time.
Here are some different kinds.

16

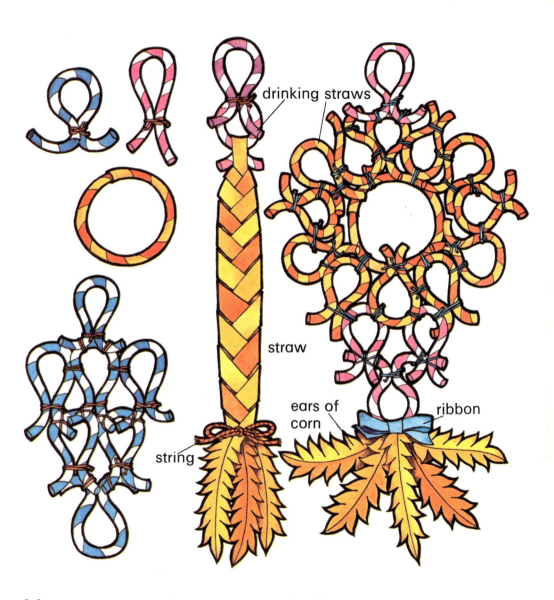

drinking straws

straw

ears of corn

ribbon

string

You can make a corn dolly
with drinking straws.
What ways can you join them together?

17

cereal

margarine

left-overs

bread

water

cheese

nuts

lard

Winter

Make some pudding for the birds.
Put bread and fat in a bowl.
Mix in left-overs and a little water.

18

Put the pudding outside.
Put out some water in a dish.
You can watch the birds come and eat
if you stay very quiet.

Cut Christmas tree shapes out of card.
Make two slits like this.
Slide the two parts together.
Now decorate the Christmas trees.

20

Make a Christmas log
to decorate the table.
Put holly and berries around it.
Ask a grown-up to light the candle.

Seasons words

branches
(page 2)

sandpit
(page 8)

buds
(page 2)

sandcastle
(page 9)

nest
(page 4)

plants
(page 9)

stall
(page 7)

wall-
hanging
(page 11)

harvest
(page 12)

straws
(page 17)

mask
(page 14)

slit
(page 20)

lanterns
(page 14)

holly
(page 21)

corn dolly
(page 16)

berries
(page 21)

Remember

If you are picking blackberries
it is best to wear gloves
to protect your hands.

Never eat berries
you do not know well.
Ask a grown-up first.

Keep away from birds' nests,
especially in spring.
This is when there may be
eggs in the nest.
If you frighten the mother
she may leave the eggs.

Seasons come at different
times of the year
in different parts
of the world.
In Europe Christmas comes
in winter;
but in Australia
it is midsummer at Christmas.
Many Australians
spend Christmas Day
on the beach.

24

Some harder projects

Easter eggs

Decorated eggs make lovely presents at Easter. Boil eggs in water for about 8 minutes. Then put them in cold water to cool them. When they are cold you can paint them in bright colours and patterns. You could stick decorations on too. Cover the egg in glue. Stick on sequins, coloured paper, silver paper or small pieces of material. Stick on anything you can find that would look nice. Put straw or crêpe paper in a basket. Lay the eggs on top.

Summer parasol

You will need a very big piece of paper for this. Wallpaper lining paper or an old roll of wallpaper would be best. Cut a piece of paper about 60 centimetres wide and $1\frac{1}{2}$ metres long. Paint it with patterns or pictures. Make a fold across the paper five centimetres from the end. Turn the paper over. Now make another fold five centimetres wide next to the first one. Go on doing this all along the paper, folding first in one direction and then the other. Fold up the paper and fix one end together tightly with sticky tape. Fix a stick to this end with sticky tape. Bend round the two corners at the other end until they meet. Fix them together with sticky tape. Now your parasol is ready to use.

25

Some harder projects

Autumn jewellery

Look for things like nuts, conkers, acorns, chestnuts, seeds, dried ferns and corn. Sort them into colours that go well together. Try to find different sizes too. Use a sharp needle and some strong thread. Thread the things you have found. Tie some coloured wool or ribbon on the ends. You could fix more than one row of autumn 'beads' together to make a pretty bracelet.

Christmas candlesticks

You will need some potatoes and silver foil to make these candlesticks. Cut a slice off the bottom of each potato. This makes a flat base. Then cut a hole in the top of each potato. Make it just big enough to stick a candle in. Ask a grown-up to help you with this. Wrap the potatoes in silver foil. Press the foil into the hole at the top. Put a blob of thick Polyfilla paste into each hole and stick a candle into it. Fix on pieces of holly and berries. Tie coloured ribbons round the candlesticks. These candlesticks would look lovely on the Christmas dinner table.